Muffin Mania

Cathy Prange & Joan Pauli

www.muffinmania.ca

binding brilliance
publishing

Muffin Mania®
by Cathy Prange and Joan Pauli

Third Printing of the New Edition November 2008

Published and Distributed by
Binding Brilliance Publishing
PO BOX #31055 725 College St.
Toronto, Ontario, Canada
M6G 4A7

Printed by Astley Gilbert
Toronto, Ontario

Cover Photograph by Meredith McRae
Layout Design and Illustrations by Meredith McRae

I.S.B.N. 978-0-9810295-0-4

Printed in Canada

To our Mother

Her love of baking inspired us to share this collection with muffin lovers everywhere.

● ● ●

The original introduction to
Muffin Mania when it was first published in 1982:

Muffins - A sign of the Times
A Healthy Alternative to Junk Food!

Every Friday morning is muffin baking time in our kitchens - got to get ready for the week-end, you know! Well, after years and years of making the same old family favourites, we decided it was time for a change, so we searched through our books and magazines and started baking.

Naturally, we met with a few disasters in dry, hard, tasteless muffins. However, we weren't about to give up. Back to the kitchen we went. One by one we cut down on this, added a dash of that, and the result is the most mouth-watering collection of recipes that you can find.

You do not require a degree in Home Economics, and you need not attend a gourmet cooking class. Nothing could be simpler! These recipes are tried and proven through hours and hours of pure muffinery. Our families and friends can attest to each and every one of these recipes. We owe them a great deal of thanks for putting up with our muffin madness and other insanities, for what must have seemed like a thousand muffins. Also, a special thanks to our muffin-tasting gal-friends, who gave us great encouragement to put out this collection together.

So muffin lovers! Pull out your muffin tins, turn the page to that muffin taste you always drooled for, and start baking. In fact, you'll get so excited with these muffin capers that when your friends arrive for coffee, the first thing you'll hear is m-m-m-muffins!

Sisters, Partners and Friends
Cathy Prange
Joan Pauli

**I would like to thank the authors, my grandmother
& her sister Joan.**

Grandma, you are an intelligent woman
with the best sense of humour and I really appreciate all your
love and support. I wish I could thank my Aunt Joannie;
however she passed away at the age of fifty-five. Not only will she
be remembered for the success of the *Mania* cookbooks, but also
for her warm, fun loving nature and as a loving wife and
wonderful mother to her three sons.

- Martha Prange

Publisher, Granddaughter and Muffin Lover

Following in My Grandmother's Footsteps

When my grandmother, Cathy Prange, and her sister, Joan Pauli, wrote this cookbook twenty-five years ago they had no idea how successful it would become. Cathy and Joan, already best friends, soon became business partners. I have always looked up to my grandmother. I remember giving a presentation to my grade six Home Economics class on *Muffin Mania*. I felt so proud to stand up in front of my class and talk about my grandmother's cookbook. To me she was a celebrity. Ten years later, my grandmother has encouraged me to republish the first cookbook in the *Mania* series, *Muffin Mania*.

The overwhelming success of *Muffin Mania* encouraged Cathy and Joan to write more. *Nifty Nibbles* (now *Nibble Mania*), a collection of appetizers, finger foods, and snacks followed within a year. *Veggie Mania*, consisting of easy to prepare soups, salads, and veggie casseroles was published in the year I was born. Our family has always loved sweets, so the sisters compiled their favorite recipes for fellow sweet lovers, and launched *Sweet Mania*. This volume contains recipes for delicious pies, cakes, mouthwatering desserts, cookies, squares, and some of my very favorite Christmas goodies and other festive treats.

The *Mania* series was an instant sensation in Canada and beyond. When *Muffin Mania* went out of print, my grandmother was besieged by a constant deluge of letters. Muffin lovers everywhere expressed an ardent desire to purchase copies for a generation that had been raised on these classic recipes. Our family has enjoyed reading your letters and hearing your stories. Your fond memories of *Muffin Mania* increase the many pleasures of placing Joan and Cathy's book back into print.

Martha Prange
July 2008

Hints

1. We use pre-sifted, all purpose flour. If using cake and pastry flour, you will need ¼ cup more.

2. Muffins, like tea biscuits, should be mixed as quickly and lightly as possible; stir only to moisten. Batter should look lumpy. If using an electric mixer for blending, use for only the liquid ingredients

3. We have baked most of our muffins at 375° F, as too hot an oven results in tough, leathery muffins. However, everyone's oven in different, so judge for yourself!

4. If you like big, beautiful muffins, fill tins to the top. Grease the top of the tins as well as the inside for easy unmolding.

5. If you have trouble unmolding fruit filled muffins, let muffins cool completely before unmolding.

6. All these muffins freeze beautifully. To freeze, cool completely, wrap in foil and put in air-tight plastic bags. To reheat, unwrap and bake at 350° F in oven or toaster oven. Soft, moist and hot – 10 min. Crusty – 15 min.

7. To sour 1 cup of milk or cream, add 1 tbsp. vinegar or lemon juice.

8. Fill any unused muffin cups halfway with water to prevent warping of the pan and/or over-browning of the muffins.

9. We have suggested canola oil in our recipes, however other vegteable oils can be used.

10. Never serve a cold muffin!

Basic Muffin Batter or The Nothing Muffin

1 c. all purpose flour
2 tsp. baking powder
½ tsp. salt
½ c. white sugar
¼ c. melted butter or margarine
1 egg, beaten
½ c. milk

Stir together dry ingredients.

Add melted butter and beaten egg to milk.

Add liquid ingredients to dry, stirring only to moisten.

To this batter, add anything you have on the shelf -
chocolate chips, butterscotch chips, peanut butter chips, fruit,
nuts, etc.

Or add nothing and serve with your scrambled eggs for breakfast
with your favourite jam or jelly.

Fill greased muffin cups.

Bake at 375° F for 15-20 min.

* Yields – 8 medium muffins.

Contents

Breakfast

Coffee Break

Lunch-Brunch Muffins Instead of Bread

Tea Time

Muffins for Dessert

Oh, by the way! While we have suggested different times of the day to enjoy your muffin, each one is perfect for any occasion, according to your taste.

Breakfast

Lorna's Apple Muffins

¼ c. shortening or margarine
¾ c. white sugar
½ tsp. vanilla
1 egg, beaten
1 c. all purpose flour
1 tsp. baking soda
¼ tsp. salt
½ tsp. cinnamon
¼ tsp. nutmeg
1 ½ c. chopped apples
1 tbsp. cream

Cream shortening and sugar. Add vanilla and beaten egg.

Stir together dry ingredients and add, stirring just to moisten.

Add apples and cream gently.

Fill greased muffin cups and bake at 350°F for 20-25 minutes.

Batter is very thick and these muffins do not rise high but are moist and delicious!

* Yields- 8-9 muffins.

Apple Muffins without cheese are like a kiss without a squeeze! Why not try 1 cup of grated old cheddar in these?

MARTHA'S NOTES

Cathy and Joan always told their friends how easy it was to make muffins. When they talked about writing a cookbook, their husbands thought it would just be talk. Little did they know that *Muffin Mania* would soon become a best seller!

Apple Cinnamon Muffins

½ c. butter, softened, or margarine
¾ c. white sugar
1 egg, beaten
1 c. buttermilk
1 tsp. salt
1 ½ c. diced apples
1 c. all purpose flour
¾ c. whole wheat flour
1 tsp. baking soda
1 tsp. cinnamon

Topping
1 tsp. cinnamon
2-3 tbsp. white sugar

Blend butter, sugar and egg until smooth.

Add buttermilk, salt, apples and mix well.

Stir together flour, baking soda and cinnamon and add, stirring only to moisten.

Spoon into greased muffin cups and sprinkle with topping.

Bake at 375°F for 20 minutes.

* Yields – 10 large muffins

- - - - - - - - - - - - - - - - - - - MARTHA'S NOTES - - - - - - - - - - - - - - - - - - -

Cathy and Joan both had three children. My Aunt Karen shares her love of baking with my grandma. She has suggested some tips on how to lighten up some of her favourite muffin recipes in this book. *Smart cookies eat lighter muffins!*

Karen's tips to lighten this muffin:
1. Reduce the amount of butter or margarine to ¼ cup.
2. Reduce the amount of white sugar to ⅔ cup. The topping will make the muffins sweet enough!

Applesauce Bran Muffins

1 c. All Bran cereal
¼ c. milk
1 c. applesauce
⅓ c. canola oil
1 egg
1 ½ c. all purpose flour
3 tsp. baking powder
½ tsp. baking soda.
½ tsp. salt
1 tsp. cinnamon
⅓ c. brown sugar

Stir All Bran, milk, applesauce, oil, and egg together.

Stir together the dry ingredients.

Add bran mixture to dry ingredients, stirring just to moisten.

Fill greased muffin cups and bake at 375°F for 15-20 minutes.

* Yields – 10 large muffins

Raisins or nuts or both may be added to this batter.

4

Applesauce Oatmeal Muffins

1 c. all purpose flour
3 tsp. baking powder
½ tsp. cinnamon
½ tsp. salt
¼ tsp. nutmeg
¾ c. rolled oats (regular or instant)
¼ c. brown sugar
1 egg
¼ c. canola oil
⅓ c. milk
⅔ c. applesauce

Mix dry ingredients well with a fork.

Beat egg, then add oil and milk.

Stir in applesauce.

Stir this into the dry ingredients, mixing only until moistened.

Spoon into greased muffin cups and bake at 375°F for 20 minutes.

* **Yields – 10 large muffins**

Applesauce Raisin Muffins

4 eggs
2 c. white sugar
1 ½ c. canola oil
1 ¾ c. applesauce
3 c. all purpose flour
1 tbsp. cinnamon
2 tsp. baking powder
2 tsp. baking soda
1 tsp. salt
2 c. raisins

Beat eggs slightly. Add sugar, oil and applesauce and beat thoroughly.

Add dry ingredients and blend until smooth.

Stir in raisins.

Fill greased muffin cups ⅔ full and sprinkle brown sugar on the top of batter.

Bake at 375°F for 15-20 minutes.

* **Yields – 18-24 good size muffins**

Best Ever Banana Muffins

2 c. mashed bananas (4 -5 med.)
¾ c. white sugar
1 egg
⅓ c. melted butter or margarine
1 tsp. baking soda
1 tsp. baking powder
½ tsp. salt
1 ½ c. all purpose flour

Mash bananas. Add sugar and slightly beaten egg.

Add the melted butter.

Add the dry ingredients.

Fill greased muffin cups and bake at 375°F for 20 minutes.

* Yields – 9 large muffins

This is our families' very favourite!

- - - - - - - - - - - - - - - MARTHA'S NOTES - - - - - - - - - - - - - - - -

This is truly one of our families' favourite muffins! My Aunt Jan has baked these so many times for my cousins Catie and Jackie that her recipe page is completely worn out. We love to add chocolate chips to make them even more delicious. Try adding 1 cup. chocolate chips.

Karen's tips to lighten this muffin:
1. Reduce the amount of butter or margarine to ¼ cup.
2. Reduce the amount of white sugar to ⅔ cup.

Banana Oatmeal Muffins

1 c. rolled oats
1 c. milk
2 c. all purpose flour
½ c. white sugar
1 tsp. salt
5 tsp. baking powder
1 tsp. baking soda
½ tsp. cinnamon
¼ tsp nutmeg
½ c. butter or margarine, melted and cooled
2 eggs
2 tsp. vanilla
2 c. mashed bananas (4 – 5 med.)

Combine oats and milk and set aside.

In large bowl, mix flour, sugar, salt, baking powder, baking soda, cinnamon and nutmeg.

To soaked oat mixture, add melted margarine, eggs, vanilla and bananas.

Add wet mixture to dry ingredients and stir only until the flour is moistened.

Fill greased muffin cups and bake at 375°F for 20 minutes.

* **Yields – 14-18 large muffins**

MARTHA'S NOTES

Karen's tips to lighten this muffin:
1. Reduce the amount of butter or margarine to ¼ cup
2. Aunt Karen never hesitates to reduce the number of eggs.

Whole Wheat Banana

1 c. mashed bananas (2-3 med.)
⅔ c. brown sugar
⅓ c. canola oil
2 eggs
¾ c. all purpose flour
¾ c. whole wheat flour
1 tsp. baking powder
1 tsp. baking soda
½ tsp. salt

Topping
¼ c. white sugar
½ tsp. cinnamon

Combine bananas, brown sugar, oil and eggs. Mix well.

Stir dry ingredients together and add to banana mixture, mixing to combine.

If desired, ½ cup chopped nuts may be added to the batter.

Spoon into well-greased muffin cups. Sprinkle topping on muffins and bake at 350°F for 20 minutes.

* Yields – 10 large muffins

Using whole wheat flour adds extra texture, flavour and fiber.

- - - - - - - - - - - - - - - MARTHA'S NOTES - - - - - - - - - - - - - -

Joan's son Mark came home one day to find their kitchen overflowing with the latest muffin creations and called it a "mania of muffins." The authors then knew that the perfect name for their book would be "Muffin Mania."

Crunchy Bran Muffins

1 c. buttermilk
1 tsp. baking soda
½ c. butter or margarine
¾ c. brown sugar
1 egg
1 tbsp. molasses
1 c. natural bran
1 c. all purpose flour
¼ tsp. salt
¼ c. each raisins or currants, finely chopped nuts and dates

Combine buttermilk and baking soda and set aside.

Cream butter and brown sugar thoroughly. Add egg and beat well.

Add buttermilk and soda, then molasses and bran. Blend.

Combine flour and salt and stir in. Fold in fruit and nuts.

Spoon into well-greased muffin cups and bake at 375°F for 20 minutes or until done.

* Yields - 9 large muffins

This recipe was sent to us by our sister-in-law from the cottage country. It proved to be one of our favourites!

- - - - - - - - - - - - - - - - MARTHA'S NOTES - - - - - - - - - - - - - - -

Karen's tips to lighten this muffin:
Reduce the amount of butter or margarine to ¼ cup.

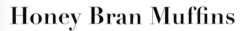

Honey Bran Muffins

1 c. natural bran
1 c. buttermilk
⅓ c. butter or margarine
½ c. brown sugar
2 tbsp. honey
1 egg
1 c. all purpose flour
2 tsp. baking powder
½ tsp. baking soda
1 tsp. salt

Soak bran in buttermilk while preparing the rest.

Cream butter and brown sugar. Beat in the honey and egg. Add the bran and buttermilk.

Stir together the flour, baking powder, baking soda and salt.

Add dry ingredients to wet mixture and stir until moistened.

Fill greased muffin cups and bake at 375°F for 15-20 minutes.

* Yields – 9 large muffins

- MARTHA'S NOTES - - - - - - - - - - - - - - - - - - -

Aunt Karen likes to add raisins to this recipe when she is baking for her husband Bob.

Karen's tips to lighten this muffin:
Reduce the amount of butter or margarine to ¼ cup.

Mother Milner's Old-Fashioned Bran Muffins

¼ c. shortening
¾ c. brown sugar
1 egg
1 c. natural bran
½ c. sour milk
1 scant tsp. baking soda
1 c. all purpose flour
1 tsp. baking powder
Pinch salt

Cream shortening and sugar and add the egg and beat.

To sour ½ cup of milk, add ½ tbsp. vinegar or lemon juice.

Dissolve the soda in the milk, add the bran.

Add flour, baking powder and salt.

Fill greased muffin cups and bake at 375°F for 15- 20 minutes.

Dates may be added. Cook the dates with a little water and let them cool. Mix the date mixture with flour before adding to batter.

* Yields – 8 large muffins

As kids we used to pour maple syrup over these for dessert. M-m-good!

- - - - - - - - - - - - - - - - - - - MARTHA'S NOTES - - - - - - - - - - - - - - -

In newspaper articles from 1982, Cathy and Joan credit their success to their mother, 81-year old Cora Milner of Kitchener. She taught them to make bran and banana muffins when they were little girls. Cora and her best friend, Thelma Thorn, often accompanied the authors on their promotional tours.

Mrs. Bun's Bran Muffins or Pail Full of Muffins

2 c. boiling water
2 c. All Bran cereal
1 c. butter or margarine
3 c. white sugar
3 tbsp. brown sugar
4 eggs
1 qt. buttermilk
5 c. all purpose flour
3 tbsp. baking soda
1 tbsp. salt
4 c. bran flakes
2 c. raisins or chopped dates

Pour boiling water over All Bran and let stand.

In very large bowl (or bath tub), cream butter, sugars and eggs. Add buttermilk and then bran mixture. Stir until blended.

Stir together the flour, baking soda and salt, and add to above mixture. Mix well.

Add bran flakes and fold in just until moist. Add raisins or dates.

Chill 1 day before baking.

Spoon into well-greased muffin cups and bake at 375°F for 15-20 minutes.

This recipe makes **6 dozen muffins.** The batter may be kept 6 weeks in the refrigerator in a covered jar.

- MARTHA'S NOTES - - - - - - - - - - - - - - - - -

In the News! - 1982
More Muffin Mania piping hot off the press.
Just Talking: by Frances L. Denney
"If you have a lot of hungry mouths to feed, you can't go wrong with Mrs. Bun's Bran Muffins, also called Pail Full of Muffins because the recipe makes six dozen. You can mix the batter in a very large bowl, or as the sisters suggested, in the bathtub."

Christmas Morning Cranberry Muffins

1 c. cranberries
¼ c. white sugar
1 ½ c. all purpose flour
¼ c. white sugar
2 tsp. baking powder
1 tsp. salt
½ tsp cinnamon
¼ tsp. ground allspice
1 beaten egg.
¼ tsp. grated orange peel
¾ c. orange juice
⅓ c. melted butter or margarine
¼ c. chopped walnuts

Coarsely chop cranberries.

Sprinkle with ¼ c. sugar and set aside.

In bowl, stir together flour, ¼ c. sugar, baking powder, salt, cinnamon, and allspice, and make a well in the center.

Combine egg, orange peel, orange juice and melted butter. Add all at once to the flour mixture, stirring to moisten.

Fold in cranberry mixture and nuts.

Fill greased muffin cups and bake at 375°F for 15-20 minutes or until golden.

* Yields – 9 large muffins

MARTHA'S NOTES

Karen's tips to lighten this muffin:
Reduce the amount of butter or margarine to ¼ cup.

Date Muffins

1 c. chopped dates
1 tsp. baking soda
¼ c. margarine or shortening
1 c. boiling water
1 cup lightly packed brown sugar
1 well-beaten egg
1 c. bran
1 tsp. baking powder
1 c. all purpose flour

Combine dates, baking soda and margarine. Pour boiling water over this and let cool.

Combine sugar and egg, and add to cooled date mixture.

Stir together bran, baking powder and flour, and add to date mixture.

Stir to moisten.

Fill greased muffin cups and bake at 375°F for 15-20 minutes.

* Yields – 8 large muffins

- MARTHA'S NOTES -

In preparation for the cookbook, the authors tested a wide variety of recipes for about six months. With all this muffin creating they found themselves with bags full of muffins, so they had a muffin party for all their friends - their toughest critics.

Sonja's Date Muffins

1 c. chopped dates
1 c. hot water
1 c. brown sugar
1 tsp. lemon juice
1 egg
1 tsp. salt
1 tbsp. canola oil
1 ½ c. natural bran
¾ c. all purpose flour
1 tsp. baking soda
1 c. sour milk or buttermilk

Mix dates, hot water, ½ c. of the brown sugar and lemon juice and simmer until thickened.

Measure remaining brown sugar, egg, salt, oil and date filling into one bowl. Beat vigorously until smooth.

Add bran.

Add flour and baking soda, then milk. Stir only to moisten ingredients.

Spoon into greased muffin cups and let stand for 3 minutes.

Bake at 375°F for 20 minutes.

* Yields – 10 large muffins

---- MARTHA'S NOTES ----

Once Cathy and Joan had tested all their muffins they compiled a book of 63 mouth-watering muffin recipes. They went to a local printer in Kitchener, Ontario and in June 1982, *Muffin Mania* was ready for sale.

Health Food Muffins

1 ¼ c. all purpose flour
2 tsp. baking powder
2 c. granola
¼ c. brown sugar
1 tsp. salt
⅓ c. canola oil
1 c. milk
1 tsp. vanilla
⅓ c. molasses

Mix together dry ingredients.

Blend oil, milk, vanilla and molasses.

Pour mixture over dry ingredients and stir only to moisten.

Spoon into well-greased muffin cups, sprinkling more granola on the top.

Bake at 375°F for 15 – 20 minutes.

* **Yields – 10 large muffins**

Marmalade Muffins

Peel of 1 grapefruit and 1 orange
1 ½ c. buttermilk
1 c. white sugar
1 tsp. salt
½ c. butter or margarine
1 ¾ c. all purpose flour
2 tsp. baking powder
½ tsp. baking soda

Cut complete grapefruit and orange skins into blender.

Pour in buttermilk and grind until fine.

Add sugar, salt and margarine and blend.

Stir dry ingredients together in a bowl and pour rind mixture over, stirring just to moisten flour.

Fill greased muffin cups and bake at 375°F for 20 minutes.

* Yields – 12 large muffins

Light, bittersweet- a real hit for breakfast or coffee breaks!

For a slightly sweeter taste, while warm, dip in melted butter and white sugar. Absolutely scrumptious!

- - - - - - - - - - - - - - - - - MARTHA'S NOTES - - - - - - - - - - - - - -

Did you know that buttermilk is lower in fat than regular milk? The fat from the milk is removed to make butter, so don't shy away from recipes that call for buttermilk!

Oatmeal Muffins

1 c. rolled oats (regular or instant)
1 c. boiling water
½ c. butter or margarine
1 ½ c. brown sugar
2 eggs
¾ c. dates, finely chopped, or 1 c. raisins
1 c. all purpose flour
1 tsp. baking soda
1 tsp. salt
1 tsp. vanilla

Mix rolled oats and water and let stand for 20 minutes.

Cream butter and sugar.

Add eggs and beat well.

Add the dates to the dry ingredients, then add to creamed mixture.

Stir in the vanilla.

Gently fold in the oatmeal mixture.

Spoon into well-greased muffin cups and bale at 375°F for 20 – 25 minutes.

* **Yields – 10 large muffins**

A handful of coconut added to this batter makes a nice variation.

- MARTHA'S NOTES - - - - - - - - - - - - - - - - - - -

Karen's tips to lighten this muffin:
1. Reduce the amount of butter or margarine to ¼ cup.
2. Cut down the amount of brown sugar in this recipe, try 1 cup.
   instead.

Oatmeal Orange Muffins

½ c. orange juice
½ c. boiling water
1 c. rolled oats (regular or instant)
½ c. butter or margarine
½ c. white sugar
½ c. brown sugar
2 eggs
1 c. raisins
1 tsp. vanilla
1 c. all purpose flour
1 tsp. baking powder
1 tsp. baking soda
1 tsp salt

Combine orange juice and water. Add rolled oats and soak for 15 minutes.

Meanwhile, cream margarine and sugars. Beat eggs and stir in oat mixture. Stir in raisins and vanilla.

Add flour, baking powder, baking soda and salt.

Stir until moistened. Pour into well-greased muffin cups.

Bake at 375°F for 20 minutes.

* **Yields – 10 large muffins**

Pioneer Muffins

3 eggs
⅓ c. brown sugar
⅔ c. canola oil
¼ c. molasses
2 c. natural bran
1 c. grated carrots
1 c. applesauce, mashed bananas or puréed fruit
1 ½ c. liquid (water, milk, or apple juice)
1 ½ c. whole wheat flour
½ c. wheat germ
1 tsp. baking soda
2 tsp. baking powder
1 tsp. salt
1 tbsp. powdered milk
½ c. raisins (optional)

If using applesauce, add 2 tsp. cinnamon to dry ingredients and
1 c. chopped walnuts.

In a large bowl, beat eggs. Add sugar, oil, molasses, bran, carrot,
applesauce and liquid. Stir well.

In medium bowl, mix well whole wheat flour, wheat germ, baking
soda, baking powder, salt, powdered milk and raisins (if using).

Add dry ingredients all at once to egg mixture, stirring only until
moistened.

Fill greased muffin cups and bake at 375°F for 20-25 minutes.

This is a very moist, health food muffin.

Makes 2 dozen muffins.

Zucchini Muffins

2 c. all purpose flour
1 c. brown sugar
2 tsp. baking soda
2 tsp. cinnamon
⅛ tsp. nutmeg
⅛ tsp. ginger
⅛ tsp. allspice
½ tsp. salt
2 c. grated zucchini
1 apple, peeled, cored and grated
½ c. chopped nuts
3 eggs
1 c. canola oil
2 tsp. vanilla

In a large bowl, combine flour, sugar, baking soda and spices.

Stir in zucchini, apple and nuts.

In another bowl, beat eggs, oil and vanilla.

Stir into flour mixture until batter is just combined.

Spoon into well-greased muffin cups, filling to the top.

Bake at 350°F for 20 minutes.

* **Yields – 14 large muffins**

MARTHA'S NOTES

Cathy and Joan approached gift shops, book and kitchen stores about selling *Muffin Mania* and within two months sold the first 2,000 copies.

● ● ● ● ● ● ● ● ● ● ● ● ● ●

Coffee Break

Apricot Oatmeal Muffins

1 ¼ c. rolled oats (regular or instant)
1 c. all purpose flour
⅓ c. white sugar
1 tbsp. baking powder
½ tsp. salt
⅔ c. milk
1 jar (4 ½ oz.) apricot puree (baby food)
1 egg
¼ c. canola oil
1 tsp. vanilla
½ c. chopped dried apricots
⅓ c. raisins

Measure first five ingredients in large bowl and mix well.

Mix milk, apricot puree, egg, oil and vanilla in another bowl.

Add wet ingredients to dry and stir just until moistened.

Fold in apricots and raisins.

Fill greased muffin cups 2/3 full and bake at 350°F for 20 minutes.

* **Yields – 8-9 large muffins.**

- - - - - - - - - - - - - - - - - - - MARTHA'S NOTES - - - - - - - - - - - -

In 1982, articles about *Muffin Mania* started to appear in local newspapers in Kitchener Waterloo. The sisters started gaining recognition for their unique cookbook. Before long they would appear on national television and radio shows!

Carrot Nut Muffins

1 c. white sugar
¾ c. canola oil
2 eggs
1 tsp. baking soda
1 tbsp. warm water
1 tsp. vanilla
1 ½ c. all purpose flour
½ tsp. salt
1 tsp. baking powder
1 c. walnuts
1 c. grated carrots

Beat sugar, oil, and eggs.

Dissolve baking soda in water and add to egg mixture, along with vanilla. Mix well.

Add flour, salt and baking powder and mix until moistened.

Stir in nuts and grated carrots.

Bake at 375°F for 15-20 minutes.

* Yields - 9-10 large muffins

Also good with currants, raisins, quartered maraschino cherries, orange or lemon rind or cut peel. Your left-over Christmas fruit is ideal!

- - - - - - - - - - - MARTHA'S NOTES - - - - - - - - - - -

Karen's tips to lighten this muffin:
Reduce the amount canola oil to ½ cup.

Carrot Pineapple Muffins

1 c. white sugar
⅔ c. canola oil
2 large eggs, beaten
1½ c. all purpose flour
2 tsp. baking powder
1 tsp. baking soda
1 tsp. cinnamon
½ tsp. salt
1 c. finely grated carrots
1 c. crushed pineapple, drained
1 tsp. vanilla

In beater bowl, combine sugar, oil and beaten eggs.

In another bowl, combine flour, baking powder, baking soda, cinnamon and salt and mix well.

Add dry ingredients to the sugar and oil mixture, and stir to moisten.

Add grated carrots, pineapple, and vanilla.

Fill greased muffin cups to the top and bake at 375°F for 20 minutes.

* **Yields 9 - 10 large muffins.**

Chopped nuts may be added, if desired.

MARTHA'S NOTES

Karen's tips to lighten this muffin:
Reduce the canola oil to ¼ of a cup.

Carrot Wheat Muffins

1 c. all purpose flour
½ c. whole wheat flour
2 tsp. baking powder
½ tsp. salt
¼ c. brown sugar
½ tsp. cinnamon
⅛ tsp. all spice
1 c. carrots, coarsely grated
1 tsp. grated orange rind
1 egg
1 c. milk
¼ c. molasses
¼ c. melted butter or margarine
½ c. raisins
¼ c. chopped nuts

Measure dry ingredients into large bowl. Mix well.

Stir in carrots and orange rind.

In small bowl, beat egg with milk, molasses and melted butter.

Add to dry ingredients all at once, stirring just to moisten.

Fold in raisins and nuts.

Fill greased muffin cups ¾ full.

Bake at 375°F for 20 minutes.

* **Yields – 10 large muffins**

Honey - Carrot - Date Muffins

¼ c. butter or margarine
½ c. honey
½ c. milk
2 eggs
1½ c. all purpose flour
1 heaping tsp. baking powder
1 tsp. salt
1 c. grated carrots
1 c. chopped, pitted dates

Melt butter and honey. Stir in milk and eggs. Beat.

Combine dry ingredients and stir thoroughly.

Stir in liquid mixture and fold in carrots and dates.

Bake at 375°F for 15-20 minutes.

* Yields – 10 large muffins

Delicious when heated and served with butter, cream cheese or marmalade!

Coffee Date Muffins

1 c. dates, chopped
½ tsp. cinnamon
⅔ c. strong, hot coffee
⅔ c. shortening or margarine
1 c. brown sugar
2 eggs
1 ½ c. all purpose flour
1 tsp. baking powder
½ tsp. baking soda
½ tsp. salt

Icing
½ c. icing sugar
1 tbsp. coffee

Combine dates, cinnamon and coffee, and let stand 20 minutes. to soften dates.

Cream shortening and sugar. Add 1 egg at a time and beat after each addition.

Add date mixture.

Mix dry ingredients together and add, stirring just to moisten.

Fill greased muffin cups and bake at 375° F for 20 minutes.

Combine icing sugar and coffee. Ice muffins when slightly cooled.

* **Yields – 9-10 large muffins**

----------------------- MARTHA'S NOTES -----------------------

Cathy and Joan were among the first in a trend of do-it-yourself cookbook authors. They wrote, published and marketed *Muffin Mania* from scratch, turning these Canadian homemakers into entrepreneurs.

Coffee Walnut Muffins

1 tbsp. instant coffee granules
½ c. hot water
½ c. whole milk or cream
1 egg, beaten
½ c. melted shortening or canola oil
1 ½ c. all purpose flour
3 tsp. baking powder
⅓ c. white sugar
1 tsp. salt
½ c. chopped walnuts

Dissolve coffee granules in hot water and add the milk, beaten egg and shortening.

Stir flour, baking powder, sugar, and salt together, and stir in the walnuts.

Pour liquid ingredients into the dry and mix only to moisten.

Spoon into greased muffin cups and bake at 375°F for 15-20 minutes.

* **Yields – 9 large muffins**

Gingersnap Raisin Muffins

¼ c. butter or margarine
¼ c. white sugar
1 egg
½ c. molasses
1 c. all purpose flour
1 tsp. baking soda
¼ tsp. salt
½ tsp. cinnamon
½ tsp. ginger
¼ tsp. cloves
½ c. hot water
1 c. raisins

Cream margarine and sugar. Add sugar and molasses and beat.

Stir together flour, baking soda, salt, cinnamon, ginger and cloves.

Stir into molasses mixture. Gradually add the hot water and stir until smooth.

Stir in raisins.

Fill greased muffin cups and bake at 375°F for 20 minutes.

* Yields- 8-9 large muffins

- - - - - - - - - - - - - - - MARTHA'S NOTES - - - - - - - - - - - -

After the first printing, people started showing up on the author's doorsteps seeking copies of *Muffin Mania*. Mail orders arrived daily. A little hand-written note was returned with each book and Cathy and Joan would sign the first page of every copy.

Morning Glory Muffins

2 c. all purpose flour
1 ¼ c. white sugar
2 tsp. baking soda
2 tsp. cinnamon
½ tsp. salt
2 c. grated carrots
½ c. raisins
½ c. nuts
½ c. coconut
1 apple, peeled, cored, and grated
3 eggs
1 c. salad oil
2 tsp. vanilla

In a large bowl, mix together flour, sugar, baking soda, cinnamon and salt.

Stir in carrot, raisins, nuts, coconut, and apple.

In a medium bowl, beat eggs with oil and vanilla.

Stir into flour mixture until batter is just combined.

Spoon into well-greased muffin cups, filling to the top.

Bake at 350°F for 20 minutes.

Makes about 14 large, scrumptious muffins!

Aunt Dorothy raved about these! She thought we should call them "Heavenly Hash"

- - - - - - - - - - - - - - - - - - - MARTHA'S NOTES - - - - - - - - - - - - - -

Karen's tips to lighten this muffin:
1. Reduce the amount of oil to ½ cup.
2. Use 2 eggs instead of 3 eggs.

Orange Date Muffins

1 whole orange
½ c. orange juice
½ c. chopped dates
1 egg
½ c. butter or margarine
1 ½ c. all purpose flour
¾ c. white sugar
1 tsp. baking soda
1 tsp. baking powder
½ tsp. salt

Cut the orange into pieces to remove seeds.

Drop pieces into blender with the orange juice and whirl until peel is finely chopped.

Drop in the dates, egg, and butter. Give blender a short whirl.

Stir together the dry ingredients.

Pour orange mixture over and stir only until moistened.

Fill greased muffin cups and bake at 375°F for 15-20 minutes.

* Yields 9-10 large muffins.

Raisins may be substituted for the dates for an equally delicious muffin.

- - - - - - - - - - - - - - - - - - MARTHA'S NOTES - - - - - - - - - - - - - - - - -

Karen's tips to lighten this muffin:
Reduce the amount of butter or margarine to ¼ cup.

Dallas's Oatmeal Carrot Muffins

1 c. buttermilk
1 c. quick-cooking oats (not instant)
1 egg, beaten
½ c. brown sugar
⅓ c. melted butter or margarine
1 c. finely chopped carrots
1 tsp. vanilla
Grated rind of 1 orange
1 c. whole wheat or all purpose flour
2 tsp. baking powder
1 tsp. baking soda
1 tsp. salt

Pour buttermilk over oats in bowl. Add beaten egg, sugar, melted butter, carrots, vanilla and orange rind, and mix thoroughly.

Combine flour, baking powder, baking soda, and salt. Add to oat mixture, stirring just until moistened.

If desired, add raisins or dates at this point.

Fill greased muffin cups and bake at 375°F for 15-20 minutes.

* **Yields- 9-10 large muffins.**

MARTHA'S NOTES

Muffin Mania started making its way across the country. Cathy received a letter all the way from the Northwest Territories. An Inuvik resident found the book in a remote nursing station. They made muffins with powdered eggs and dried fruit!

Peanut Butter Muffins (Cory's Favourite)

1 ½ c. all purpose flour
½ c. white sugar
2 tsp. baking powder
½ tsp. salt
½ c. chunky peanut butter
¼ c. butter or margarine
1 c. milk
2 beaten eggs

Mix dry ingredients and cut in peanut butter and butter until mixture is crumbly.

Add milk and eggs and stir until moistened.

Fill greased muffin cups and sprinkle with mixture of chopped peanuts and sugar.

Variation:
Instead of sprinkling topping before baking, after baking, while muffins are hot, brush tops with melted jelly and dip in chopped peanuts.

Bake at 375°F for 15-20 minutes.

* Yields 9-10 large muffins

Super for the little folk!

MARTHA'S NOTES

My friend Cory made these muffins for us at the cottage. Our guests raved about these muffins, making this old recipe a new favourite!

Pumpkin Muffins

4 eggs
2 c. white sugar
1 ½ c. canola oil
1 ¾ c. pumpkin (small can)
3 c. all purpose flour
1 tbsp. cinnamon
2 tsp. baking powder
2 tsp. baking soda
1 tsp. salt
2 c. raisins

Beat eggs slightly. Add sugar, oil and pumpkin and beat thoroughly.

Add dry ingredients and mix until smooth.

Stir in raisins.

Fill greased muffin cup ⅔ full and sprinkle tops with brown sugar.

Bake at 375°F for 15-20 minutes.

* **Yields – 18-24 good-size muffins.**

This is a good fall muffin for Oktoberfest or Thanksgiving!

MARTHA'S NOTES

Aunt Karen sometimes substitutes the raisins for shredded carrots.

Karen's tips to lighten this muffin:
1. Reduce the amount of canola oil to 3/4 cup.
2. Cut down on the eggs, using only 3 eggs.

Raisin Muffins

¾ c. brown sugar
½ c. shortening or margarine
1 egg
1 ¼ c. raisins
1 ¼ c. all purpose flour
1 tsp. nutmeg
1 tsp. baking soda
½ tsp. salt

Cream sugar and shortening. Add egg and beat until fluffy.

Cook raisins in 2 c. water for 20 min. Drain raisins, saving ½ c. liquid.

Add liquid to creamed mixture.

Stir dry ingredients together and add to above, stirring until moistened.

Stir in cooked raisins.

Fill greased muffin cups and bake at 375°F for 15-20 minutes.

* **Yields – 8-9 large muffins**

MARTHA'S NOTES

Cathy and Joan explained that *Muffin Mania* was a profitable venture mainly because they had done all their own marketing. The first sales of the book were made by driving around to book stores, kitchen and gift shops selling a few at a time.

● ● ● ● ● ● ● ● ● ● ● ● ● ● ●

Lunch-Brunch Muffins
Instead of Bread.

Donna's Beer Muffins

3 c. all purpose flour
5 tsp. baking powder
½ tsp. salt
3 tbsp. white sugar
1 bottle beer

Measure dry ingredients into bowl and pour beer over, stirring to blend.

Spoon into greased muffin cups and brush tops with butter.

Bake at 350°F for 15-20 minutes.

* Yields - 9 large muffins

Serve hot! A little grated cheddar cheese sprinkled on top of these before baking makes them even better.

Another Oktoberfest muffin! Serve with traditional German food-cabbage rolls, pig tails, etc.

- - - - - - - - - - - - - - - - MARTHA'S NOTES - - - - - - - - - -

In the News!
When "The Cookbook Store" in Toronto ON, celebrated their 20th anniversary they named *Muffin Mania* in their top twenty favourite books in the last twenty years and mentioned Donna's Beer Muffins! Later, for their 25th anniversary, the Cookbook Store listed *Muffin Mania* as one of their top 10 cookbooks in the Toronto Star.

Cheddar Cornmeal Muffins

1 c. all purpose flour
½ c. cornmeal
1 heaping tsp. baking powder
½ tsp. salt
Pinch cayenne
1 egg
1 c. milk
¼ c. melted butter or margarine
1 ½ c. grated old cheddar cheese

Stir together flour, cornmeal, baking powder, salt and cayenne.

Beat egg with milk and butter and add dry ingredients, stirring to moisten.

Stir in 1 c. cheese and spoon into greased muffin cups.
Sprinkle with remaining cheese.

Bake at 375°F for 15-20 minutes.

* Yields - 8 large muffins

Serve hot with butter or freeze and reheat before serving. These are delicious with homemade soups, chili or salads. For a yummy variation, add ½ c. cooked, crumbled bacon to the batter.

Cornmeal Muffins

1 c. flour
1 tbsp. baking powder
½ tsp. salt
½ c. white sugar
1 c. cornmeal
½ c. butter or margarine
1 egg
¾ c. milk

Mix dry ingredients together.

Melt butter, add egg and milk and combine well.

Stir liquid ingredients into dry ingredients and combine just until moistened.

Fill greased muffin cups and bake at 375°F for 15-20 minutes.

Serve hot!

* Yields- 8 large muffins

Variation:
Add ½ c. corn niblets or ½ c. crumbled bacon.

"An old-fashioned Waterloo Country favourite."

- - - - - - - - - - - - - - - · MARTHA'S NOTES · - - - - - - - - - - - - - -

It was apparent that *Muffin Mania* was traveling around the world. In 1983 the sisters received an order all the way from New Zealand.

Bacon Corn Muffins

½ lb. bacon
1 c. all purpose flour
1 c. cornmeal
2 tbsp. white sugar
1 tbsp. baking powder
½ tsp. salt
1 can (10 oz.) cream corn
½ c. milk
1 egg, beaten

Cook bacon until browned and crisp. Drain on paper towel and crumble. Set aside. Reserve ¼ cup bacon drippings.

Mix flour, cornmeal, sugar, baking powder and salt.

In small bowl, beat corn, milk, egg and bacon drippings.

Stir into flour mixture and fold in bacon pieces.

Bake at 375°F for 15-20 minutes or until done.

Serve warm!

* **Yields- 8 large muffins**

Cheese Bran Muffins

1 c. natural bran
1 ½ c. sour milk or buttermilk
¼ c. butter or margarine
¼ c. white sugar
1 egg
1 ½ c. all purpose flour
2 tsp. baking powder
½ tsp. salt
¼ tsp. baking soda
1 c. grated old cheddar cheese

Soak bran in sour milk.

Cream margarine and sugar. Beat in egg.

Stir together dry ingredients and add to creamed mixture alternately with the bran, starting and ending with flour mixture.

Stir in cheese.

Fill greased muffin cups and bake at 375°F for 20-30 minutes.

Serve warm!

*   **Yields- 9-10 large muffins**

MARTHA'S NOTES

In 1983, Cathy and Joan were nominated for women of the year by the Kitchener Waterloo Octoberfest Women's Committee.

Cheese and Ginger Muffins

1 ½ c. all purpose flour
2 tsp. baking powder
½ tsp. baking soda
1 tsp. ground ginger
½ tsp. salt
Dash cayenne
¼ c. butter or margarine
1 egg, beaten
½ c. milk
½ c. corn syrup
1 c. grated old cheddar cheese

Mix dry ingredients in bowl.

Melt margarine. Add beaten egg, milk and corn syrup and mix well. Combine dry ingredients with egg mixture and mix until moistened.

Stir in grated cheese.

Fill greased muffins cup and bake at 375° for 15-20 minutes.

* Yields - 9 large muffins

If desired, sprinkle tops with more grated cheese before baking. Serve hot!

Cheese and Onion Muffins

1 ½ c. all purpose flour
1 tbsp. baking powder
1 tbsp. white sugar
1 c. grated old cheddar cheese
1 pkg. onion soup mix
1 c. milk
1 egg
¼ c. canola oil

Stir together dry ingredients and stir in the cheese.

Combine soup mix and milk. Let stand 5 minutes.

Beat egg, milk mixture and oil and add to dry ingredients, mixing lightly just to combine.

Spoon into well-greased muffin cups and bake at 375°F for 15-20 minutes.

Serve hot!

* Yields- 9 large muffins

These were a big hit at our Muffin Tasting Luncheon!

- - - - - - - - - - - - - - - - MARTHA'S NOTES - - - - - - - - - - - - - - - -

By 1984, *Muffin Mania* sales surpassed 160,000 copies. In the book's 16th printing, they were approaching the 200,000 mark!

Mushroom Muffins

1 egg
1/3 c. melted shortening or oil
1/4 c. milk
1 can (10 oz.) condensed cream of mushroom soup (undiluted)
1 1/2 c. all purpose flour
3 tsp. baking powder
1/4 tsp. salt
2 tbsp. cut up parsley or chives (optional)

Beat the egg and blend in shortening, milk and soup.

Stir together flour, baking powder and salt.

Add liquid ingredients to the dry along with parsley or chives, stirring only until moistened.

Fill greased muffin cups and bake at 375°F for 15-20 minutes.

Serve warm!

* Yields- 9 large muffins

We don't know why you couldn't make these with any tin of cream soup.

Sandy's Seafood Muffins

1 c. small shrimp, drained and coarsely chopped
¼ c. grated old cheddar cheese
⅓ c. sour cream
¼ c. finely chopped celery
1 ½ c. all purpose flour
2 tbsp. white sugar
2 tsp. baking powder
½ tsp. salt
¼ tsp. thyme
1 egg
¾ c. milk
⅓ c. canola oil

Combine shrimp, cheese, sour cream and celery. Set aside.

In bowl, stir flour, sugar, baking powder, salt and thyme.

Make a well in center of dry ingredients.

In bowl, slightly beat the egg with a fork, and beat in milk and oil. Add dry ingredients and stir just until moist.

Spoon into well-greased muffin cups and top with about 1 tbsp. of the shrimp mixture.

Bake at 375°F for 20 minutes. Garnish with snipped parsley, if desired.

Serve warm.

* Yields- 8-9 large muffins

For a more economical muffin, try tuna or salmon instead of shrimp.

Tea Time

Blueberry Muffins

1¾ c. all purpose flour
½ c. white sugar
3 tsp. baking powder
½ tsp salt
1 c. blueberries
1 egg
1 c. milk
½ c. melted butter or margarine

Stir together dry ingredients and add blueberries.

Combine egg, milk and melted butter and stir into flour mixture and blueberries, stirring just to moisten. Do not beat.

Fill greased muffin cups and bake at 375°F for 20 minutes.

* **Yields- 10 large muffins**

For a nice flavour, add the grated rind of one orange or lemon and while hot, dip in melted butter and sugar.

- - - - - - - - - - - - - - - MARTHA'S NOTES - - - - - - - - - - - - - -

We added blueberry jelly and a sprinkle of granola to these muffins when we photographed them for the book's cover. It was a great presentation and they tasted delicious!

Karen's tips to lighten this muffin:
Reduce the amount of butter or margarine to ¼ cup.

Blueberry Oatmeal Muffins

1 c. all purpose flour
2 tsp. baking powder
½ tsp. salt
½ tsp cinnamon
¾ c. rolled oats (regular or instant)
½ c. lightly packed brown sugar
1 egg
1 c. milk
¼ c. melted butter or margarine
¾ c. fresh or frozen blueberries

Stir dry ingredients together.

Beat together, in large bowl, egg, milk and melted margarine.

Add the dry ingredients and stir just until moistened.

Fold in blueberries.

Fill greased muffin cups and bake at 375°F for 20 min. or until brown.

* **Yields- 8 large muffins**

This recipe was sent to us by a friend from the West. She uses Saskatoon berries. We think elderberries or any other local fruit in season would be delicious.

- - - - - - - - - - - - - - - - - - MARTHA'S NOTES - - - - - - - - - - - - - - - - - -

My cousin Maggie likes these muffins with a cinnamon and sugar topping. Sprinkle topping on tops of muffins before baking.

Topping
1 tsp. cinnamon
2-3 tbsp. white sugar

Cherry Muffins

½ small bottle maraschino cherries
1 ½ c. all purpose flour
½ c. white sugar
2 tsp. baking powder
½ tsp. salt
milk
2 eggs
3 tbsp. melted butter or margarine

Drain cherries, reserving liquid. Cut up cherries.

Stir together dry ingredients and add the cherries.

Add milk to reserved cherry juice to make 1 cup liquid. Add eggs and butter.

Stir the liquid ingredients into the flour mixture, stirring just to moisten.

Fill greased muffin cups and bake at 375°F for 15-20 minutes.

* Yields- 9-10 large muffins

- - - - - - - - - - - - - - - - - - - MARTHA'S NOTES - - - - - - - - - - - - - - - -

Cathy and Joan were receiving mail from *Mania* fans around the world. *Muffin Mania* was a hit! In an interview, Cathy said that the book was not written by qualified cooks because they weren't *writing* for qualified cooks.

Joye's Lemon Tea Muffins

1 c. all purpose flour
½ c. white sugar
1 heaping tsp. baking powder
1 tsp. salt
¼ c. butter or margarine
½ c. fresh lemon juice
2 eggs
Finely grated rind of 1 lemon

Topping
¼ c. melted butter
1 tbsp. lemon juice
½ c. white sugar

Combine dry ingredients and blend well.

Melt butter. Remove from heat and stir in lemon juice, eggs and lemon rind.

Stir egg mixture into dry ingredients and stir only to moisten.

Fill greased muffin cups and bake at 375° F for 15-20 minutes or until nicely browned.

To prepare topping, combine melted butter and lemon juice. Measure sugar in separate dish. Remove muffins from pan while warm and dunk top of muffins into butter, then sugar.

* **Yields- 8-9 large muffins**

A cup of raisins or 1 tbsp. poppy seeds added to this batter makes this a pleasurable muffin for any time of the day.

Lemonade Muffins

1 ½ c. all purpose flour
¼ c. white sugar
2 ½ tsp. baking powder
½ tsp. salt
1 beaten egg
1 can (6 oz.) frozen lemonade, thawed (⅔ cup)
¼ c. milk
⅓ c. canola oil
½ c. chopped walnuts

Mix dry ingredients.

Combine egg, ½ c. lemonade, milk and oil.

Add to dry ingredients and stir just until moistened.

Gently stir in nuts.

Fill greased muffin cups and bake at 375°F for 15-20 minutes or until done.

While hot, brush with remaining lemonade and sprinkle with white sugar.

* **Yields- 8-9 large muffins**

MARTHA'S NOTES

A newspaper article from a 1984 interview with Cathy and Joan said that somebody had told the sisters that they were responsible for the muffin craze that was sweeping Canada. *Muffin Mania* was even translated into French - *La Manie des Muffins*.

Maple Walnuts Muffins
(Harry's Favorite)

1 c. all purpose flour
½ c. whole wheat flour
2 tsp. baking powder
1 tsp. salt
½ tsp. cinnamon
¼ c. butter or margarine
⅓ c. pure maple syrup
⅔ c. milk
1 egg
½ tsp. maple extract
½ c. chopped walnuts

Topping
2 tbsp. white sugar
¼ tsp. cinnamon
3 tbsp. finely chopped nuts

In bowl, combine dry ingredients.

Melt butter. Add syrup and milk, then beat in egg and maple extract.

Stir butter mixture into dry ingredients and stir to moisten.

Stir in walnuts.

Combine topping ingredients and sprinkle on top of muffins.

Fill greased muffin cups and bake at 375°F for 15-20 minutes.

* **Yields- 8 large muffins**

Muffins That Taste Like Donuts (Meredith's Favorite)

1¾ c. all purpose flour
1½ tsp. baking powder
½ tsp. salt
½ tsp. nutmeg
¼ tsp cinnamon
⅓ c. canola oil
¾ c. white sugar
1 egg
¾ c. milk

Topping
½ c. melted butter or margarine
⅓ c. white sugar
1 tsp. cinnamon

In a bowl, combine flour, baking powder, salt, nutmeg and cinnamon.

In another bowl, combine thoroughly oil, sugar, egg, and milk.

Add liquid ingredients to dry and stir only to combine.

Spoon into well-greased muffin cups and bake at 350°F for 20-25 minutes.

Shake muffins out immediately when done and while hot, dip in melted butter, then sugar and cinnamon. For another variation, fill tins ½ full with batter, add 1 tsp. jam and top with the rest of the batter.

* **Yields- 8-9 large muffins**

- - - - - - - - - - - - - - - - MARTHA'S NOTES - - - - - - - - - - - - - - -

My friend Meredith (this edition of *Muffin Mania*'s cover and layout designer) loves this recipe. Her mother told us that when she was pregnant with Meredith she made every muffin in this book. I wonder where Meredith gets her sweet tooth from?

Rich, Delicious Orange Tea Muffins

1 ½ c. all purpose flour
½ c. white sugar
2 tsp. baking powder
½ tsp. salt
½ c. butter or margarine
½ c. fresh orange juice
2 eggs
Grated rind and juice of 1 orange
1 tsp. sugar

Combine flour, sugar, baking powder and salt and blend well.

Melt butter. Take off heat and stir in orange juice, eggs and orange rind. Beat.

Stir liquid into dry mixture and blend just until moistened.

Spoon into greased muffin cups. Soak 1 tsp. sugar in orange juice and spoon on top of batter.

Bake at 375°F for 15-20 minutes or until done.

* **Yields- 8-9 large muffins**

A handful of coconut or raisins added to this batter would also be delicious!

MARTHA'S NOTES

By 1985, articles about *Muffin Mania* started popping up in newspapers in the United States. Cathy and Joan's muffins were making it across North America!

Sour Cream Muffins

1 egg
1 c. sour cream
¼ c. milk
1 ½ c. all purpose flour
2 tbsp. white sugar
1 tsp. baking powder
½ tsp. baking soda
1 tsp. nutmeg
1 tsp. salt
½ c. raisins (optional)

Beat egg. Stir in sour cream and milk.

Stir dry ingredients together and blend into liquid.

Fold in raisins, if using, and spoon into well-greased muffin cups.

Bake at 375°F for 15-20 minutes.

* **Yields- 8-9 large muffins**

Sour Cream Pineapple Muffins

¼ c. white sugar
1 egg
¼ c. butter, softened, or margarine
1 c. sour cream
1½ c. all purpose flour
1 tsp. baking powder
½ tsp. baking soda
½ tsp. salt
1 c. well-drained, crushed pineapple.

Measure sugar, egg, soft butter and sour cream into bowl and beat.

Stir together flour, baking powder, baking soda and salt and blend.

Add cream mixture to dry ingredients and stir until moistened.

Stir in pineapple to mix.

Fill greased muffin cups and bake at 375°F for 15-20 minutes.

* **Yields - 8-9 large muffins**

- - - - - - - - - - - - - - - **MARTHA'S NOTES** - - - - - - - - - - - - - - -

The sisters thought that the best part about writing cookbooks was the letters they received from fans. *Muffin Mania* fans loved the homespun recipes. Cathy and Joan even received letters from places as far away as Nigeria, Germany, and Saudi Arabia!

Muffins for Dessert

Chocolate Cheesecake Muffins

1 pkg. (4 oz.) cream cheese, softened
2 tbsp. plus ½ c. white sugar
1 c. all purpose flour
3 tbsp. unsweetened cocoa powder
2 tsp. baking powder
½ tsp. salt
1 beaten egg
¾ c. milk
⅓ c. canola oil

In small bowl, beat cream cheese and 2 tbsp. of the sugar until light and fluffy. Set aside.

In large bowl, stir together flour, remaining ½ c. sugar, cocoa, baking powder and salt.

Make a well in center of dry ingredients. Combine egg, milk and oil. Add all at once to dry ingredients, stirring just until moistened. (Batter should be lumpy.)

Spoon about 2 tbsp. of chocolate batter into each greased muffin cup or paper cup. Drop 1 tsp. of cream cheese mixture on top and then add more chocolate batter.

Bake at 375°F for 20 minutes.

Dust with powdered sugar, if desired.

* Yields - 8 large muffins

Our friend, Fanny, a chocolate "nut", liked these the best of all!

- MARTHA'S NOTES - - - - - - - - - - - - - - - - -

Granny Fanny has been my grandmother's best friend for seventy years! The two met when they were around seven years old.

Chocolate Chip Muffins

1½ c. all purpose flour
½ c. white sugar
3 tsp. baking powder
¼ tsp. salt
1 c. chocolate chips
1 egg
1 c. milk
⅓ c. melted butter or margarine

Mix dry ingredients and add chocolate chips.

Combine egg, milk and butter and stir into flour mixture.
Do not beat.

Bake at 375°F for 20 minutes.

A few chocolate chips melted and drizzled over the tops when muffins are slightly cooled make these a special dessert treat for chocolate lovers.

* Yields- 9 large muffins

Our Cadet, Bob, from Robert Land Academy, always requests these when he's home on week-end leaves.

- - - - - - - - - - - - MARTHA'S NOTES - - - - - - - - - - - - -
By 1985, *Muffin Mania* sold 265,000 copies (5,000 of them in French).

Jam Filled Muffins

1 ½ c. all purpose flour
¼ c. white sugar
2 tsp. baking powder
½ tsp. baking soda
½ tsp. salt
¼ c. butter or margarine
1 c. plain yogurt
¼ c. milk
1 egg
½ tsp. vanilla
Jam or jelly

Blend dry ingredients.

Melt butter. Take off heat and stir in yogurt and milk and blend. Beat in egg and vanilla.

Add butter mixture to dry ingredients and stir until moistened.

Spoon half of the batter into well-greased muffin cups. Place about 1 tsp. raspberry jam or jelly in each muffin and top with remaining batter.

Bake at 375°F for 15-20 minutes.

*   **Yields- 9 large muffins**

Dust with confectioner's sugar before serving, if desired.

Maple Syrup Muffins (Heavenly)

¼ c. butter or margarine
½ c. white sugar
1 tsp. salt
1 ¼ c. all purpose flour
2 tsp. baking powder
¾ c. rolled oats (regular or instant)
½ c. milk
½ c. maple syrup

Glaze
1 tbsp. butter, softened
½ c. icing sugar
1 tbsp. maple syrup

Soften margarine and blend in sugar and salt.

Add flour and baking powder and blend with pastry cutter until crumbly. Mix in oats.

Blend milk and syrup together in measuring cup and pour over dry ingredients, stirring only to moisten.

Bake at 350°F for 20 minutes.

Spread glaze over when slightly cooled

* Yields- 8 large muffins

MARTHA'S NOTES

With the success of *Muffin Mania*, Cathy and Joan went on to write three more books: *Nibble Mania*, *Veggie Mania*, and *Sweet Mania*. Over 750,000 Mania books were sold!

Mincemeat Rum Muffins

1 ½ c. all purpose flour
¼ c. white sugar
2 tsp. baking powder
½ tsp. salt
½ c. butter or margarine
½ c. apple juice
2 eggs
1 c. mincemeat (canned)
1 tsp. sugar
¼ c. rum

Combine dry ingredients and blend well.

Melt margarine and stir in apple juice and eggs. Beat well.

Stir liquid ingredients into dry mixture.

Add mincemeat and stir until moistened.

Spoon into greased muffin cups. Soak 1 tsp. sugar in rum and spoon on top of batter.

Bake at 375°F for 15-20 minutes.

* **Yields- 8-9 large muffins**

A delicious muffin for the Christmas season!

Pina Colada Muffins

½ c. white sugar
1 egg
¼ c. butter or margarine
1 c. sour cream
1 tsp. rum extract
1½ c. all purpose flour
1 tsp. baking powder
½ tsp. baking soda
½ tsp. salt
1 small can crushed pineapple, drained
½ c. coconut

Measure sugar, egg, margarine, sour cream and rum extract and beat until blended.

Stir together dry ingredients and add, stirring until barely blended.

Add pineapple and coconut.

Bake at 375°F for 20 minutes.

* **Yields 8-9 large muffins**

Winnie's Rhubarb Muffins

1 ¼ c. all purpose flour
1 ½ tsp. baking powder
1 tsp. salt
¼ c. white sugar
¼ c. brown sugar
1 large egg
½ c. milk
¼ c. canola oil
1 tsp. almond flavouring
1 ½ c. diced rhubarb

Mix dry ingredients.

Beat egg, add milk, oil and almond flavouring.

Pour egg mixture over dry ingredients and stir to moisten.

Fold in rhubarb. Sprinkle tops with sugar before baking.

Bake at 375°F for 20 minutes.

* Yields - 8 large muffins

Variation:
Instead of sprinkling sugar on muffins before baking, dip tops of warm muffins in sugar after baking.

Peaches or other fruit in season are just as delicious!

- - - - - - - - - - - - - - - - MARTHA'S NOTES - - - - - - - - - - - - - -

When *Muffin Mania* went out of print and there were no books left for sale, letters with *Muffin Mania* requests started pouring in. Cathy started photocopying her personal copy to send to her most desperate fans.

Rhubarb Pecan Muffins

2 c. of all purpose flour
¾ c. of sugar
1 ½ tsp. baking powder
½ tsp. baking soda
1 tsp. salt
¾ c. of chopped pecans
1 egg
¼ c. of vegetable oil
2 tsp. of grated orange peel (optional)
¾ cup orange juice
1 ¼ c. of finely chopped rhubarb

In a large bowl combine flour, sugar, baking powder, baking soda, salt and pecans.

In a medium bowl beat the egg. Add the oil, orange juice and orange peel (if using).

Add all at once to the flour mixture and stir just until the batter is moist.

Stir in the rhubarb.

Fill lightly greased muffin cups with the batter.

Bake at 350° oven for 25 to 30 minutes.

* Yields - 8 large muffins

- - - - - - - - - - - - - - - MARTHA'S NOTES - - - - - - - - - - - - - - -

This is a new recipe! My grandmother loved Aunt Jan's recipe for her Rhubarb Pecan Muffins!

Index